grilling

simple and delicious recipes that
are easy to make in your grill pan

Bernice Hurst

p

This is a Parragon Publishing Book
This edition published in 2004

Parragon Publishing
Queen Street House
4 Queen Street
Bath, BA1 1HE, UK

Copyright © Exclusive Editions 2002

ISBN: 1-40543-641-7

Printed in China

Produced by
THE BRIDGEWATER BOOK COMPANY LTD

Photographer: Trevor Leak
Home Economist: Marianne Lamb

Cover Photography: Calvey Taylor-Haw
Home Economist: Ruth Pollock

NOTES FOR THE READER

- This book uses imperial, metric, and cup measurements. Follow the same units of measurement throughout; do not mix imperial and metric.

- All spoon measurements are level: teaspoons are assumed to be 5 ml, and tablespoons are assumed to be 15 ml.

- Unless otherwise stated, milk is assumed to be whole milk, eggs and individual vegetables such as potatoes are medium, and pepper is freshly ground black pepper.

- Recipes using raw or very lightly cooked eggs should be avoided by infants, the elderly, pregnant women, convalescents, and anyone suffering from an illness.

- The times given are an approximate guide only. Preparation times differ according to the techniques used by different people and the cooking times may also vary from those given. Optional ingredients, variations, or serving suggestions have not been included in the calculations.

contents

introduction

Grilling is an age-old method of cooking that has recently enjoyed a resurgence in popularity as a quick and easy way of creating attractive and delicious dishes. It is ideal for entertaining and for making nibbles. If you want to focus on the flavor of just one or two excellent ingredients, then this is one of the best methods to use. While any sauces have to be prepared separately rather than used to cook the main ingredients, the opportunity to use marinades and contrasting dressings or accompaniments more than compensates for this.

Some planning is required: for example, some skewers will be too long, those with handles may not fit in your pan, and when using wooden sticks, you should first soak them in water for half an hour to prevent burning. Toothpicks make excellent skewers for grilled miniature canapés, as do sprigs of rosemary or lemongrass.

lemon-grilled salmon
page 16

seared duck breast
page 52

The very essence of the grilling method is to create charred and blackened surfaces to the food you are preparing. Successful grilling entails heating the pan until it is very, very hot and then searing the surface of the food you are cooking over as high a heat as it can stand.

Be aware that grilling can be a smoky process, so we recommend that you shut all internal doors and open external windows and doors to help with ventilation.

Key to Recipes

easy

Recipes are graded as follows:
1 spoon = easy;
2 spoons = very easy;
3 spoons = extremely easy.

serves 4

Recipes generally serve four people. Simply halve the ingredients to serve two, taking care not to mix metric and imperial measurements.

15 minutes

Preparation time. Where marinating or soaking are involved, these times have been added on separately: eg, 15 minutes + 30 minutes to marinate.

40 minutes

Cooking time. Cooking times do not include the cooking of side dishes or accompaniments served with the main dishes.

grilled bell pepper & zucchini salad
page 64

fruit kabobs
page 74

Fish and grilling make an ideal combination, bringing out the flavor and texture of the fish to perfection. There is such a wide range of fresh or frozen fish available today that it should be possible to find something to please everyone. More than any other ingredient, however, fish must be as fresh as possible when prepared and eaten. The simple addition of lemon or lime juice and fresh herbs is usually quite sufficient, but vegetables can transform a basic dish into something quite exquisite.

fish & seafood

angler fish kabobs

very easy   serves 4

15 minutes   10–15
+ 1 hour to   minutes
marinate

ingredients

1 lb 10 oz/750 g angler fish fillet, skinned
  and bonded

MARINADE
¼ cup vegetable oil, plus extra for basting
1 tsp paprika

1 red onion, cut into 8 pieces
8 white mushrooms
1 red or green bell pepper, seeded
  and cut into 8 pieces
2 zucchini, cut into 8 thick slices

4 tomatoes, halved, to garnish

Cut the angler fish into bite-size cubes. Place in a glass dish, pour the oil over it, and sprinkle with paprika. Mix well. Cover the dish with plastic wrap and refrigerate for at least 1 hour.

Remove the angler fish from the refrigerator and bring back to room temperature. Select skewers that will fit on your grill pan. Soak wooden skewers in water for 30 minutes to prevent them from burning. Preheat the grill over moderate heat.

Assemble the kabobs, threading pieces of fish alternated with the vegetable pieces. Place the kabobs on the griddle and cook for 10–15 minutes, turning frequently and basting occasionally with oil, or until the fish is firm and the vegetables tender. If you wish, place the tomato halves on the grill pan for the last 2–3 minutes.

Serve the kabobs on individual serving plates, garnished with raw or cooked tomato halves.

whole grilled fish

easy   serves 4

10 minutes   10–15
+ 1 hour   minutes
to rest

ingredients

4 tbsp chopped fresh mint
4 tbsp chopped fresh parsley
4 tbsp chopped fresh tarragon
4 x 12 oz/350 g trout, herring, or sea bass,
   cleaned and gutted
salt and pepper
juice of 1 lemon

4 tbsp butter, diced
1 tbsp oil or butter, for brushing

TO SERVE
new potatoes
green beans with almonds

Mix the herbs together in a small bowl. Place one quarter of the mixture in the cavity of each fish, reserving a small amount for serving. Gently press the fish closed.

Make 2–3 shallow cuts on each side of the fish. Sprinkle with salt, pepper, and half of the lemon juice. Rub in well and let the fish rest for 1 hour.

Preheat the grill over medium heat. Spray or brush with oil or melted butter.

Dot the fish with half of the diced butter, then place it, buttered-side down, on the grill. After about 6 minutes, when the bottom is brown and crispy, sprinkle the remaining lemon juice on top, dot with the remaining butter, and turn to cook the second side.

Transfer the cooked fish to individual plates and serve with boiled new potatoes and green beans with almonds.

seafood brochettes

very easy   serves 4

5 minutes   10–15 minutes

ingredients

4 scallops, cleaned

4 baby squid, cleaned

4 jumbo shrimp, in their shells

4 white mushrooms

4 cherry tomatoes

4 baby corn cobs (optional)

2 tbsp vegetable oil, for basting

a few sprigs of fresh flatleaf parsley,
   to garnish

buttered rice, to serve

Select skewers that will fit on your grill pan. If using wooden skewers, soak them in water for 30 minutes to prevent them from burning. Preheat the grill pan over medium heat.

Meanwhile, assemble the kabobs, threading several pieces of all 3 types of seafood and the vegetables alternately on each.

Place the kabobs on the grill pan and cook for 5–10 minutes, turning frequently and basting occasionally with oil, or until the fish is firm and the vegetables are tender. Be very careful not to overcook the squid (which will make it tough).

Remove the kabobs from the grill pan and transfer to individual serving plates. Garnish with parsley and serve with buttered rice.

lime-basted tuna steaks

ingredients

extremely easy   serves 4

5 minutes
+ 30 minutes
to marinate   5 minutes

4 x 4½ oz/125 g fresh tuna steaks,
  sliced thinly

MARINADE
juice of 1 lime
2 tbsp vegetable oil

mixed salad greens, to serve

Arrange the tuna steaks in a single layer in a shallow dish.

To make the marinade, combine the lime juice and oil in a small bowl. Whisk well, then pour the marinade over the fish. Cover the dish with plastic wrap and refrigerate for 30 minutes.

Preheat the grill pan over high heat. Remove the fish from the refrigerator and bring back to room temperature. Drain off the marinade and pat the fish dry with paper towels.

Place the tuna on the grill pan and sear quickly, then turn, and sear the second side. Reduce the heat to medium and cook for 3 minutes longer, or until the fish is firm but still pink inside.

Remove the fish from the grill pan and serve immediately with mixed salad greens.

lemon-grilled salmon

ingredients

very easy   serves 4

5 minutes   10–15
minutes

2 lb/900 g salmon fillet, cut into
  4 pieces
juice of 1 lemon

¼ cup butter, diced
salt and pepper

sprigs of fresh parsley or dill, to garnish

Preheat the grill pan over high heat.

Sprinkle the fish with lemon juice, dot with butter, and season with salt
and pepper.

Place the salmon on the hot grill pan, skin-side down. Cook for 10–15 minutes,
turning once when the first side is brown and crusty. The exact cooking time will
vary, depending on the thickness of the fillet. When it is ready, the fish should be
firm and flake easily with a fork.

Transfer the salmon to a serving dish and serve with sprigs of fresh parsley or dill,
arranged around the fish to garnish.

caribbean lobster skewers

easy   serves 4

15 minutes   10–15 minutes

ingredients

2 cooked lobsters or lobster tails
1 small pineapple
1 red bell pepper, seeded and
   cut into 8 pieces
4 shallots, cut into fourths
¼ cup butter, melted

TO SERVE
sautéed potatoes
salad greens

Select skewers that will fit on your grill pan. If using wooden skewers, soak them in water for 30 minutes to prevent them from burning.

Remove the lobster meat from its shell, cut into large chunks, and set aside. Skin the pineapple, then cut lengthwise into quarters. Remove the hard core and cut each wedge into quarters.

Preheat the grill pan over moderate heat while you assemble the kabobs. Thread each skewer with several pieces of lobster alternated with pineapple, bell pepper, and shallots. Brush the kabobs with the melted butter.

Cook on the grill pan for 10–15 minutes, depending on the size of the pieces, or until the lobster is thoroughly heated and the vegetables tender. Turn frequently and baste occasionally.

Remove the kabobs from the grill pan and transfer to individual serving plates. Serve with sautéed potatoes and salad greens.

jumbo shrimp with lemon & lime leaf

very easy   serves 4
as a starter

5 minutes   10 minutes
+ 1 hour
to marinate

ingredients

12 large jumbo shrimp

MARINADE
2 scallions, chopped finely
juice of ½ lemon
1 tsp fresh chopped lime leaf
1 tsp red chili, seeded and chopped finely
    or 1 tsp dried hot chili flakes

TO SERVE
garlic mayonnaise
lemon wedges

Place the shrimp in a large mixing bowl. Add the marinade ingredients and mix well. Cover the bowl with plastic wrap and refrigerate for 1 hour.

Preheat the grill pan over high heat and remove the shrimp from the refrigerator.

Cook the shrimp for 2–3 minutes on each side, turning once and ensuring that the shells are crispy and well browned.

Transfer the shrimp to a large serving dish. Serve immediately with a bowl of garlic mayonnaise and lemon wedges.

seared chili mint scallops

very easy   serves 4

15 minutes 5 minutes
+ 30 minutes
to marinate

ingredients

16–24 scallops, detached from shells
  and cleaned

MARINADE
2 tbsp vegetable oil
2 tsp fish sauce
juice of ½ lime
1 garlic clove, crushed
1 small fresh chili, seeded and
  chopped finely

2 tbsp chopped fresh basil leaves
1 tbsp chopped fresh mint leaves
½ tsp fresh chopped lime leaf

TO SERVE
mixed salad greens
2 tbsp olive oil and 1 tbsp lemon juice
  (mixed), for salad dressing
fresh croûtons or Tomato Basil Bruschetta
  (see page 58)

Place the scallops in a large glass dish. Combine all the marinade ingredients in a mixing bowl. Stir until they make a thick paste. Pour over the scallops and turn gently to coat. Cover the dish with plastic wrap and refrigerate for at least 30 minutes.

Preheat the grill pan over high heat. Remove the scallops from the refrigerator and bring back to room temperature. Drain well and pat dry with paper towels.

Place the scallops on the grill pan and cook over high heat for 1–2 minutes, or until well seared. Turn and cook the second side for 1–2 minutes. Be careful not to overcook.

Remove the scallops and carefully arrange them on individual serving plates. Garnish with mixed salad greens, sprinkled with a simple olive oil and lemon juice dressing. Sprinkle with croûtons or serve with Tomato Basil Bruschetta.

tasty thai fish patties

easy   serves 4

10 minutes   5 minutes
+ 30 minutes
to chill

ingredients

2 lb 4 oz/1 kg cod, haddock, whiting,
    or coley fillet, skinned, or a mixture
1 small onion
1 small fresh chili, seeded (optional)
6–8 tbsp fresh bread crumbs
1 egg
2 tbsp fish sauce
juice of ½ lime
1 tbsp finely chopped fresh lemongrass
2 tsp finely grated fresh gingerroot

2 tsp chopped fresh cilantro
pinch of sugar
pinch of salt

1–2 tbsp vegetable oil, for brushing

fresh cilantro and scallions, to garnish

chili sauce or sweet soy sauce, to serve

Cut the fish into large pieces, place in a food processor with the onion and chili (if using), and chop finely. Transfer the fish mixture to a mixing bowl and add all the other recipe ingredients. Mix well. The mixture should be quite thick and stiff.

Cover the bowl with plastic wrap and refrigerate for at least 30 minutes. Remove the fish from the refrigerator and mix once more. Brush the grill pan with oil and preheat over high heat.

Form small patties from the fish mixture, place on the grill pan, and cook in batches for 3–4 minutes, or until golden, turning once. If necessary, brush the grill pan with another tablespoon of oil before cooking the next batch of patties.

Transfer the cooked patties to a serving dish and garnish with cilantro leaves and scallions. Serve warm or cold, accompanied by chili sauce or sweet soy sauce.

fennel-basted trout fillets

very easy   serves 4

10 minutes   10 minutes
+ 30 minutes
to marinate

MARINADE
4 tsp vegetable oil
juice of ½ lemon
4 sprigs fresh fennel, chopped finely
salt and pepper

4 fresh trout, filleted

GARNISH
fennel sprigs
lemon wedges

To make the marinade, combine the oil and lemon juice in a small mixing bowl and whisk together. Stir in the chopped fennel, salt, and pepper.

Place the trout fillets in a shallow glass dish. Pour the fennel mixture over them, cover the dish with plastic wrap, and marinate in the refrigerator for 30 minutes.

Heat the grill pan over medium heat. Remove the trout from the refrigerator and bring back to room temperature for 10 minutes. Transfer the trout to the grill pan and brush any remaining marinade over the fish. Cook the fillets for about 5 minutes on each side, turning once and brushing with the marinade.

Remove the trout from the grill pan and arrange on an attractive serving dish. Serve immediately, garnished with sprigs of fennel and lemon wedges.

nut-crusted halibut

extremely
easy

serves 4

5 minutes

10 minutes

ingredients

3 tbsp butter, melted

1 lb 10 oz/750 g halibut fillet

½ cup pistachio nuts, shelled and

chopped very finely

Brush the melted butter over the fish fillet.

Roll the fish in the chopped nuts, pressing down gently.

Preheat the grill pan. Cook the halibut over medium heat for approximately
10 minutes, turning once. Cooking time will depend on the thickness of the fillet,
but the fish should be firm and tender when done.

Remove the fish and any loose pistachio pieces from the heat and transfer to a
large serving platter. Serve immediately.

Grilling meat is as close to an indoor barbecue as it gets. The charred appearance and smoky flavor are almost as good when meat is seared on a grill pan as over charcoal. These dishes are incredibly quick and easy and also offer great flexibility in terms of marinades, sauces, and accompaniments. What more can you ask for at the end of a busy day?

meat & poultry

butterflied poussins

easy   serves 4

5 minutes   40 minutes

ingredients

2 poussins, Rock Cornish hens, or squab
4 tbsp extra virgin olive oil
4 sprigs fresh rosemary
2 small fresh chilies, seeded and diced
  (optional)
coarsely ground sea salt

2 sprigs of fresh rosemary,
  to garnish

mixed salad, to serve

To butterfly the birds, cut through the backbone with a very sharp knife or poultry shears, then turn the bird breast-side up on a cutting board and press hard to flatten. Do not cut all the way through. Preheat the grill pan over high heat.

Place the poussins, hens, or squab, skin-side up, on the grill pan. Brush with oil and arrange a sprig of rosemary on each of the 4 sections. Sprinkle with diced chili (if using) and sea salt.

Cook the birds for 10 minutes, or until the undersides are seared. Turn and sear the skin sides, then reduce the heat to medium. Continue cooking for 30 minutes longer, or until the juices in the legs run clear when pierced with a toothpick.

Transfer the poussins, hens, or squab to a cutting board, cut the bone through so that you have 4 halves, then arrange on an attractive serving dish, garnished with more rosemary. Serve with a mixed salad.

lemon & thyme chicken portions

very easy   serves 4

10 minutes   35–40
+ 4–6 hours   minutes
to marinate

ingredients

4 chicken portions
salt and pepper

MARINADE
1 garlic clove, crushed
8 sprigs of fresh thyme, finely chopped
juice and grated rind of 1 lemon
4 tbsp olive oil

GARNISH
lemon wedges
sprigs of fresh thyme

Arrange the chicken portions in a single layer in a shallow dish. Season to taste with salt and pepper.

Mix the marinade ingredients in a bowl, then spoon over the chicken. Cover with plastic wrap and marinate in the refrigerator for 4–6 hours or overnight. Turn the portions occasionally.

Before cooking the chicken, allow it to return to room temperature. Preheat the grill pan over high heat.

Place the chicken on the grill pan, skin-side down, and cook for 10 minutes, or until the skin is crisp and starting to brown. Turn, and brown the undersides, pressing down occasionally. Reduce the heat to medium and cook the chicken for a further 20 minutes, or until the juices of leg pieces run clear when pierced with a toothpick.

Remove the chicken, place on a warm serving dish, and serve garnished with lemon wedges and sprigs of thyme.

italian lamb chops

very easy   serves 4

5 minutes
+ 8–12
hours to
marinate

10 minutes

ingredients

4 lamb chops or 8 lamb cutlets
6 cherry or baby plum tomatoes

MARINADE
2 tsp dried oregano
juice of ½ lemon
2 tbsp extra virgin olive oil

a few fresh basil leaves, to garnish

cooked linguine or other pasta (optional),
   to serve

Arrange the lamb in a single layer in a shallow dish. Sprinkle with oregano, lemon juice, and oil. Cover the dish with plastic wrap and refrigerate overnight or for as long as possible.

About 10 minutes before cooking, remove the lamb from the refrigerator. Meanwhile, preheat the grill pan over high heat.

Place the lamb on the grill pan and sear for 2 minutes on each side. Reduce the heat and cook over medium heat for about 5 minutes longer, turning the pieces over once. If the chops are thick, you may need to allow a few extra minutes. The meat is best when it is pink inside.

Two to three minutes before the meat is ready, cook the tomatoes on the grill pan. Arrange the chops and cooked tomatoes on a large platter and serve immediately with the pasta (if using), garnished with basil leaves.

cilantro lamb kabobs

very easy   serves 4

20 minutes   15 minutes
+ 8–12
hours to
marinate

ingredients

MARINADE

1 bunch fresh cilantro, torn

1 large onion, cut into fourths

KABOBS

1 lb 10 oz/750 g boneless lamb, cubed

1 red onion, cut into fourths

2 zucchini, cut into fourths

8 cherry or baby plum tomatoes

Set aside 2 tablespoons of cilantro leaves.

Process the onion and remaining coriander in a food processor until you have a coarse, slushy mixture. Transfer to a large mixing bowl, add the lamb, and toss to coat. Cover the bowl with plastic wrap and refrigerate overnight.

Select skewers that comfortably fit your grill pan. If using wooden skewers, soak them in water for 30 minutes.

Remove the lamb from the refrigerator and stir again. Preheat the grill pan over high heat. Thread the lamb onto the skewers, alternating with the vegetable pieces. Cook for 5 minutes, then reduce the heat to medium, and cook for a further 10 minutes, or until the vegetables start to soften and the meat is cooked but still pink. Turn frequently and brush with any remaining marinade.

Serve the kabobs garnished with the reserved cilantro leaves.

middle eastern koftas

very easy   serves 4

10 minutes   10 minutes

1 lb 10 oz/750 g ground lamb or beef
1 small onion, cut into fourths
2 garlic cloves, crushed
2 tbsp chopped fresh flatleaf parsley
1 tsp coriander seeds
½ tsp cumin seeds
½ tsp whole black peppercorns
generous pinch of ground cinnamon
pinch of salt

Minted Yogurt Marinade (see page 94)

fresh mint and lemon wedges,
   to garnish

SERVING SUGGESTIONS
rice or Indian bread
cucumber yogurt raita
tomato and onion salad

Process the meat, onion, garlic, parsley, spices, and seasoning to a smooth paste in a food processor. Turn into a large mixing bowl.

Select flat skewers that fit comfortably onto your grill pan.

Take about 2 tablespoons of meat paste and roll gently between your palms to make a sausage shape. Carefully fold around the skewer. If you cannot find flat skewers, shape the meat into patties as you would for hamburgers.

Preheat the grill pan over high heat. Brush the koftas with minted yogurt marinade and cook for 10 minutes, turning carefully and basting regularly.

When the meat is cooked, transfer to a large serving platter and garnish with sprigs of fresh mint and lemon wedges. Serve with rice or Indian bread and bowls of cucumber yogurt raita and tomato onion salad.

homestyle hamburgers

easy

serves 4

5 minutes   10 minutes

ingredients

1 lb 10 oz/750 g ground beef
1 beef bouillon cube
1 tbsp ground dried onion
2 tbsp water
½ cup grated Cheddar cheese (optional)

SERVING SUGGESTIONS
4 sesame buns
tomato ketchup or chili sauce
mustard
dill pickles, sliced thinly
Bermuda onion, sliced thinly
large tomato, sliced thinly
lettuce leaves
French fries

Place the beef in a large mixing bowl. Crumble the bouillon cube over the meat, add the dried onion and water, and mix well. Divide the meat into 4 portions, shape each into a ball, then flatten slightly to make a burger shape of your preferred thickness.

Preheat the grill pan over high heat. Place the burgers on the grill pan and cook for about 5 minutes on each side, depending on how well done you like your meat and the thickness of the burgers. Press down occasionally with a flat turner or metal spatula during cooking.

To make cheeseburgers, sprinkle the cheese on top of the meat when you have turned it the first time.

Serve the burgers on toasted buns, with a selection of the accompaniments suggested above.

corned beef hash

very easy   serves 4

5 minutes   20–25 minutes

ingredients

¼ cup butter

1 small onion, chopped finely

1 cooked potato, diced

12 oz/350 g canned corned beef, diced

salad, to serve

Melt the butter over medium heat in a small skillet. Add the onion and cook for 5 minutes to soften. Stir in the potatoes and corned beef and mix well.

Preheat the grill pan over medium heat. Turn the corned beef mixture onto the grill pan and press together firmly to make one large patty or four small ones. Cook for 5–8 minutes, or until the underside is well browned, then turn, and cook the other side in the same way, making sure that the corned beef is thoroughly heated through.

Lift the hash onto individual serving plates and serve with salad.

sticky pork steaks

very easy   serves 4

5 minutes   10–15 minutes

ingredients

SAUCE
¼ cup plum, hoisin, sweet & sour,
  or duck sauce
1 tsp dark brown sugar
1 tbsp tomato ketchup
pinch of garlic powder
2 tbsp dark soy sauce

4 lean pork steaks

cooked rice and peas, to serve

Preheat the grill pan over high heat.

Combine the sauce of your choice, brown sugar, ketchup, garlic powder, and soy sauce in a small mixing bowl.

Arrange the pork steaks in a single layer on a flat dish. Brush the tops with sauce, then place the steaks, sauce, side down, on the grill pan. Cook the steaks for 5 minutes, pressing down occasionally to get dark grid marks.

Brush the upper side of the steaks with sauce, turn, and continue cooking for 5 minutes, or until dark grid marks appear.

Reduce the heat to medium and, turning once, cook the steaks for about 10 more minutes, or until they are firm and the juices run clear when pierced with a toothpick.

Transfer the steaks to a large dish and serve immediately, with the rice and peas.

sweet & sour pork kabobs

very easy   serves 4

15 minutes   15 minutes
+ 1 hour
to marinate

ingredients

1 lb/450 g boneless pork, cubed
Sweet & Sour Marinade (see page 92)
2 carrots, sliced thickly
1 small red bell pepper, seeded
  and cut into fourths
1 small green bell pepper, seeded
  and cut into fourths
2 tomatoes, halved
1 onion, and cut into fourths

SAUCE
2 tbsp cornstarch
2 tsp sugar
1 tbsp wine vinegar
2 tbsp sweet sherry
2½ cups water
3 tbsp tomato paste
8 pieces of preserved ginger, diced
2 tbsp ginger syrup

Mix the pork in a bowl with the marinade. Cover with plastic wrap and refrigerate for 1 hour, stirring occasionally. Blanch the carrots for 5 minutes in a pan of boiling water. Drain and cool.

Remove the meat from the refrigerator and stir. Drain from the marinade. Heat the grill pan over medium heat. Thread the meat and vegetables on skewers, then, turning frequently, cook the kabobs on the grill pan for 10–15 minutes, or until tender.

To make the sauce, mix the cornstarch and sugar in a small pan. Add the vinegar and sherry, stirring to eliminate lumps. Gradually add the water and tomato paste, still stirring. Mix in the ginger pieces and syrup. Cook over medium heat, stirring constantly, until it comes to a boil and thickens slightly.

Remove the kabobs and serve drizzled with a spoonful of sauce.

satay sticks

very easy   serves 4

15 minutes   25 minutes
+ 1 hour
to marinate

ingredients

4 skinless, boneless chicken breasts
   or 4 boneless pork steaks

MARINADE

2 tbsp finely chopped onion
1 garlic clove, chopped finely
2 tbsp chopped fresh cilantro
2 tbsp soy sauce
¼ tsp ground ginger
¼ tsp sugar
1 tbsp vegetable oil

PEANUT SAUCE

1 small onion, chopped finely
2 garlic cloves
1 red chili, seeded and ground
1 tbsp light brown sugar
1 tbsp vegetable oil
generous ½ cup crunchy peanut butter
1 tbsp lemon or lime juice
1 tbsp dark soy sauce
1¾ cups coconut milk

rice and fresh cilantro, to serve

Cut the meat into thin slices, about 2 inches/5 cm long. Combine the marinade
ingredients in a shallow dish. Add the meat and stir well. Cover with plastic wrap
and refrigerate for 1 hour or more.

For the sauce, blend the onion, garlic, chili, and sugar into a coarse paste in a food
processor. Cook in the oil in a small pan over medium heat for 5 minutes. Add the
remaining sauce ingredients and mix well. Bring to a boil, then simmer, and cook
until thickened slightly (about 15 minutes), stirring constantly.

Preheat the grill pan over high heat. Drain the meat and thread onto skewers.
Brush with oil and cook on the grill pan for 3–4 minutes on each side, or until the
meat is cooked through.

Serve the satay sticks on a bed of rice with fresh cilantro. Put the peanut sauce in
a small serving dish as an accompaniment.

seared duck breasts

very easy   serves 4

5 minutes   25 minutes

ingredients

4 boneless duck breasts

4 tbsp honey

2 tbsp orange juice

2 tsp soy sauce

TO SERVE

boiled potatoes

salad

Score across the skin of the duck breasts diagonally at intervals of 1 inch/2.5 cm.

Preheat the grill pan over high heat. Place the duck on the grill pan, skin-side down, and cook for 5 minutes, or until it is starting to brown. Turn, reduce the heat to medium, and cook for an additional 10–15 minutes.

While the duck is cooking, combine the honey, orange juice, and soy sauce.

Turn the duck so that it is skin-side up, spoon the sauce over it, and cook for another 5 minutes.

Transfer the breasts to a carving board and slice thinly at an angle. Arrange the slices on a serving dish. Serve immediately, with boiled potatoes or other vegetables of your choice and salad.

glazed ham steaks

easy   serves 4

5 minutes   10 minutes

4 cured ham steaks
4 tbsp dark brown sugar
2 tsp mustard powder
4 tbsp butter
8 slices pineapple

TO SERVE
baked potatoes
green beans

Preheat the grill pan over medium heat, place the ham steaks on it, and cook for 5 minutes, turning once. If you have room for only 2 steaks at a time, cook them completely and keep warm while cooking the second pair.

Combine the brown sugar and mustard in a small bowl.

Melt the butter in a large skillet, add the pineapple, and cook for 2 minutes to heat through, turning once. Sprinkle with the sugar and mustard and continue cooking over low heat until the sugar has melted and the pineapple is well glazed. Turn the pineapple once more so that both sides are coated with sauce.

Place the ham steaks on individual plates and arrange 2 pineapple slices either next to them or overlapping on top. Spoon over some of the sweet pan juices.

Serve with baked potatoes and green beans.

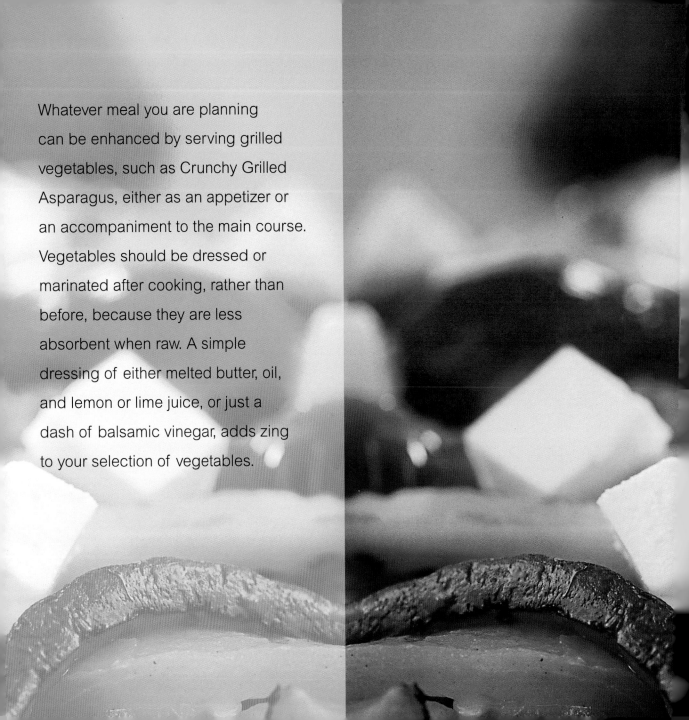

Whatever meal you are planning can be enhanced by serving grilled vegetables, such as Crunchy Grilled Asparagus, either as an appetizer or an accompaniment to the main course. Vegetables should be dressed or marinated after cooking, rather than before, because they are less absorbent when raw. A simple dressing of either melted butter, oil, and lemon or lime juice, or just a dash of balsamic vinegar, adds zing to your selection of vegetables.

vegetables

tomato basil bruschetta

extremely
easy

serves 4

10 minutes   5 minutes

1 small oval-shaped loaf of white bread
  (ciabatta or bloomer)
½ cup extra virgin olive oil
4 tomatoes
6 leaves fresh basil

salt and pepper
8 black olives, pitted and chopped
  (optional)
1 large garlic clove

Cut the bread into ½-inch/1-cm slices. Pour half of the oil into a shallow dish and place the bread in it. Stand for 2–3 minutes, turn, and stand for 2 more minutes, or until saturated in oil.

Meanwhile, seed and dice the tomatoes and place in a mixing bowl. Tear the basil leaves and sprinkle them over the tomatoes. Season with salt and pepper. Add the olives, if using. Pour in the remaining olive oil and marinate.

Preheat the grill pan over medium heat. Cook the bread until golden and crispy on both sides (about 2 minutes on each side). Remove the bread from the grill pan and arrange on an attractive serving dish.

Peel the garlic clove and cut in half. Rub the cut edge over the surface of the bruschetta. Top each slice with a spoonful of the tomato mixture and serve.

vegetable kabobs

very easy   serves 4

10 minutes   10 minutes

ingredients

4 cherry or baby plum tomatoes

2 zucchini, cut into fourths

8 white mushrooms

4 shallots, whole, peeled

2 red or green bell peppers, seeded
and cut into fourths

4 tbsp olive oil

salt and pepper

2 tbsp chopped fresh basil or oregano,
to garnish

salad greens, to serve

Select skewers that will fit comfortably on your grill pan. Soak wooden skewers in water for 30 minutes, if using.

Preheat the grill pan over high heat.

Meanwhile, arrange all the vegetables on the skewers, alternating to create a colorful selection. Brush with olive oil and season with salt and pepper.

Place the kabobs on the grill pan and cook, turning frequently, for about 10 minutes. Baste with olive oil occasionally, so that the vegetables don't dry out.

Remove the kabobs from the grill pan, arrange on a serving platter, and serve with the mixed salad greens, garnished with the chopped herbs.

grilled eggplant pâté

very easy

serves 4

10 minutes

10 minutes

ingredients

2 small eggplants
2 tbsp olive oil
juice of 1 lemon
4 tbsp tahini
2 garlic cloves, crushed (optional)

TO SERVE
carrot sticks
celery sticks
hot pita bread

Preheat the grill pan over high heat. Place the eggplants on the grill pan. Turning frequently, cook for about 10 minutes, or until the skins are black and blistered and the eggplants are very soft.

Remove the eggplants from the grill pan and cool slightly. Cut in half and scoop out the insides into a mixing bowl. Mash with a fork to make a coarse paste.

Gradually add the olive oil, lemon juice, and tahini. Stir in the garlic, if using. Mix well, tasting and adjusting ingredient amounts, until you achieve the flavor and texture you like.

Transfer the mixture to an attractive bowl and serve with sticks of raw carrots and celery, and hot pita bread.

grilled bell pepper & zucchini salad

easy

serves 4

10 minutes

20 minutes
+ 3–4 hours
to marinate

ingredients

1 red bell pepper, halved, cored and seeded

1 green bell pepper, halved, cored, and seeded

1 yellow bell pepper, halved, cored, and seeded

2 zucchini, cut into fourths lengthwise

2 tbsp olive oil, for brushing

DRESSING

2 tbsp balsamic vinegar

4 tbsp olive oil

2 tsp fresh chopped oregano

salt and pepper

4 oz/115 g feta cheese (drained weight), cubed (optional), to serve

Preheat the grill pan over high heat. Cook the bell peppers on the grill pan until the skins are blackened and the flesh is soft (about 2 minutes each side). Remove from the grill pan and wrap in damp paper towels until cool enough to handle.

Brush the zucchini pieces with oil, place on the hot grill pan, and cook until soft and well browned on both sides (about 2 minutes each side). Remove and place in a large, shallow, serving dish.

Remove the paper towels from the bell peppers and peel off the skins. Cut each piece into 4 strips and add to the zucchini. Sprinkle the vinegar and olive oil over the vegetables and mix well. Toss with the oregano. Season to taste.

Cover with plastic wrap and leave in a cool place, or in the refrigerator, for 3–4 hours. Before serving, stir through once and add the feta cheese, if using. Serve the salad at room temperature.

buttery rosemary potatoes

very easy   serves 4

10 minutes   25 minutes

ingredients

16 small new potatoes   2 tbsp fresh rosemary, chopped finely
¼ cup butter   salt and pepper

Cook the potatoes in boiling salted water for 12–15 minutes, or until just tender.
Drain well and gently rub off the skins.

Melt the butter in a large pan with the rosemary, reserving a little rosemary
to garnish.

Preheat the grill pan over medium heat.

Toss the potatoes in the melted butter until well coated. Transfer to the grill pan
and cook until golden on all sides (5–10 minutes), turning often and basting with
the rosemary butter.

Arrange the potatoes in a serving dish, sprinkle generously with salt and pepper,
and serve garnished with the reserved rosemary.

crispy sweet & white potatoes

easy   serves 4

5 minutes   20 minutes

ingredients

1 lb/450 g waxy white potatoes
1 lb/450 g sweet potatoes
generous ½ cup butter, melted
salt and pepper

TO SERVE
salad greens
dips or salsas

Preheat the grill pan over medium heat.

Thinly slice the potatoes. Brush with melted butter, then place them on the grill pan in batches, and cook for 5–10 minutes, turning once, until brown and crispy.

Transfer the first batch of cooked potatoes to a serving dish and keep warm while cooking the remainder.

Sprinkle generously with salt and pepper before serving with salad greens as an accompaniment to a fish or meat main meal, or with your favorite dips or salsas as an appetizer or as a snack with drinks.

crunchy grilled asparagus

very easy   serves 4

5 minutes   5–10
minutes

ingredients

1 lb/450 g asparagus spears, all of
  similar thickness
2 tbsp extra virgin olive oil
1 tsp coarse sea salt

juice of ½ lemon
black pepper
1 oz/25 g thinly shaved Parmesan cheese,
  (optional)

Preheat the grill pan over medium heat.

Trim the base of the asparagus spears so that they are approximately the
same length.

Arrange the asparagus in a single layer on the grill pan. Drizzle with olive oil
and sprinkle with the salt. Cook for 5–10 minutes, turning frequently. Asparagus
is particularly tasty if it gets slightly crispy as well as charred. Remove from the
grill pan and transfer to an attractive serving dish.

Sprinkle the lemon juice and black pepper over the asparagus. Serve topped with
Parmesan shavings, if using.

Hot grilled fruit is a special treat that is both juicy and crunchy at the same time. A coating of crispy browned sugar will seal in the flavor and texture of the fruit. Contrasting grilled fruit with a cold, creamy accompaniment makes the perfect end to a wonderful meal. From mouthwatering Fruit Kabobs to the sheer self-indulgence of Rum Bananas, the grilled desserts described in the following pages are deliciously tempting.

desserts

fruit kabobs

very easy   serves 4

10 minutes   10 minutes

1 lb/450 g assorted fruit (peaches,
   apricots, plums, apples, pears)
¼ cup butter, melted
2 tbsp sugar
pinch of cinnamon (optional)

SERVING SUGGESTIONS
crème fraîche
plain yogurt
ice cream

Select skewers that will fit comfortably on your grill pan. Soak wooden skewers
in water for 30 minutes, if using.

Preheat the grill pan over medium heat.

Pit the fruit as necessary, or remove cores, and cut into similar-size pieces.
Small fruit may be left whole. Arrange alternating pieces on the skewers.
Brush the fruit with melted butter.

Spread the sugar on a plate large enough to take the skewers. Mix in the
cinnamon, if using. Roll the fruit kabobs in the sugar, pressing gently to coat.

Cook the kabobs on the grill, turning occasionally. Cook for about 10 minutes,
or until the sugar has melted and started to bubble. The fruit should still be firm.

Serve hot, with crème fraîche, plain yogurt, or ice cream.

rum bananas

very easy   serves 4

1 minute   5–10
minutes

ingredients

4 bananas
4 tsp rum or Cointreau

SERVING SUGGESTIONS
sherbet
ice cream
heavy cream
crème fraîche

Preheat the grill pan over high heat.

Place the bananas, still in their skins, on the grill pan. Cook for 5–10 minutes, or until the skins are black, turning occasionally.

Remove the bananas from the grill pan, peel, and place in individual serving bowls. Pour 1 teaspoonful of rum or Cointreau over each banana and serve while still hot, with a scoop of sherbet, ice cream, heavy cream, or crème fraîche.

glazed pineapple slices

very easy   serves 4

5 minutes   5 minutes

ingredients

1 pineapple
¼ cup honey
½ cup butter, melted

SERVING SUGGESTIONS
fruit sherbet
crème fraîche
whipped cream
ice cream

mint leaves, to decorate

Peel and core the pineapple. Cut into thick slices, about 1 inch/2.5 cm wide.

Preheat the grill pan over medium heat. Meanwhile, heat the honey in a small pan over medium heat, or in a bowl in the microwave, until it is liquid.

Brush both sides of the pineapple slices with the melted butter. Place on the grill pan and cook for 2 minutes on each side, brushing with honey before and after turning so that both sides are well coated and sticky.

Remove the hot pineapple from the grill pan. Decorate with mint leaves and serve with a scoop of fruit sherbet, crème fraîche, whipped cream, or ice cream.

crunchy ginger apples

very easy   serves 4

5 minutes   10 minutes

ingredients

4 crisp, tart apples

2 tbsp lemon juice

2 tbsp butter, melted

2 tbsp raw brown sugar

4 tbsp diced preserved ginger

SERVING SUGGESTIONS

crème fraîche

whipped cream

ice cream

mint leaves, to decorate

Cut the apples in half through their circumference. Carefully remove the seeds and cores.

Place the lemon juice, butter, and raw brown sugar in 3 separate small dishes. Dip the cut side of the apples first in the lemon juice, then in the melted butter, and, finally, in the sugar.

Preheat the grill pan over medium heat. Add the apples, cut-side down, and cook for 5 minutes, or until the sugar caramelizes and the apple surfaces are dark. Turn and cook for an additional 5 minutes to blacken the skin. The cooked apples should still retain their crunch.

Arrange the apple halves in individual dishes (allowing 2 halves per serving), cut-side up, and spoon diced ginger over each half. Decorate with mint leaves and serve with a bowl of crème fraîche, whipped cream, or ice cream.

Sweet, spicy, or herbed sauces and marinades can make an enormous difference to simple grill-cooked dishes. Marinating in advance in Honey Mustard Marinade, for example, allows the flavor of herbs or spices to be absorbed before cooking. Serving a complementary dressing or sauce, such as Plum Salsa, can highlight the taste of the quickly cooked main ingredients. The flavor of the marinade or the taste and texture of the sauce should enhance the main ingredient, without distracting from it.

sauces & marinades

plum salsa

very easy

serves 4 as side dish

15 minutes

ingredients

8 plums, pitted

4 tbsp red onion, chopped finely

1 medium bunch fresh cilantro,
chopped finely

2 small fresh chilies, seeded and
chopped finely

pinch of sugar

pinch of salt

Cut the plums into bite-size chunks. Place in a large mixing bowl.

Add the onion, cilantro, chilies, and seasoning, mix well, and serve immediately.
This salsa is at its best when freshly made.

minted melon salsa

easy   serves 4 as
side dish

15 minutes   none

6 oz/175 g cantaloupe or charentais melon
4 oz/115 g cucumber

large handful of fresh mint,
finely chopped

Cut the flesh of the melon from its shell and remove all the seeds. Cut into tiny dice. Place in a large mixing bowl.

Cut the cucumber into fourths lengthwise and scrape away any seeds. Cut the flesh into tiny dice.

Add the cucumber to the melon with the mint and mix well. Let rest for 10 minutes before using.

Serve with grilled fish or poultry.

tomato cilantro salsa

very easy   serves 4 as
             a side dish

10 minutes   no cooking;
             30 minutes
             resting

ingredients

1 lb/450 g ripe tomatoes, seeded and
   cut into fourths
4 tbsp olive oil
2 tbsp red wine vinegar
2 tbsp fresh chives, chopped finely
1 medium bunch fresh arugula or sorrel,
   chopped finely

1 medium bunch fresh cilantro,
   chopped finely
pinch of sugar
salt and pepper

Cut the tomato quarters into strips and place them in a large mixing bowl.

Add the oil and vinegar to the tomatoes and mix well.

Add the chives, arugula or sorrel, and cilantro, then season to taste with sugar,
salt, and pepper and mix well. Let rest for 30 minutes before serving.

honey mustard marinade

ingredients

easy   serves 4

5 minutes   none

2 tbsp honey
2 tbsp whole-grain mustard
1 tsp ground ginger
1 tsp garlic powder

2 tsp finely chopped fresh rosemary
4 tbsp dark soy sauce
¼ cup olive oil

Combine all the ingredients, except the oil, in a small mixing bowl.

Gradually add the oil, whisking constantly, until it is fully absorbed into the mixture.

Use to marinate and baste chicken or pork, especially spare ribs.

sweet & sour marinade

extremely easy   serves 4

5 minutes   none

ingredients

1 cup orange, grapefruit, or pineapple juice
⅛ cup sweet sherry
½ cup dark soy sauce
½ cup chicken stock
¼ cup cider vinegar

1 tbsp tomato purée
¼ cup light brown sugar
1 tsp powdered garlic
1 tsp powdered ginger

Combine the fruit juice, sherry, soy sauce, chicken stock, and cider vinegar in a mixing bowl.

Stir in the tomato purée, sugar, garlic, and ginger. Mix well.

This mixture can be used to marinate and baste chicken or pork.

minted yogurt marinade

extremely easy   serves 4

10 minutes   none

2 garlic cloves, crushed
1 tsp salt
4 tbsp finely chopped fresh mint
1 cup plain yogurt

1 tsp ground cumin, coriander seeds,
  or cinnamon (optional)
1 onion (optional)

Mix the garlic with the salt to make a paste. Turn into a mixing bowl and stir in the mint, yogurt, and cumin (coriander, or cinnamon, if using).

If you are using the onion, place it in a food processor, together with the yogurt mixture, and blend for a few seconds, or until the mixture is coarse and the onion is blended in.

Use to marinate and baste lamb.

index